START-A-CRAFT

Picture Framing

Get started in a new craft with easy-to-follow projects for beginners

FAY BOON

THE APPLE PRESS

A QUINTET BOOK

Published by The Apple Press
6 Blundell Street
London N7 9BH

ISBN 1-85076-587-1

This book was designed and produced by
Quintet Publishing Limited
6 Blundell Street
London N7 9BH

Creative Director: Richard Dewing
Designer: James Lawrence
Project Editor: Anna Briffa
Editor: Lydia Darbyshire
Photographer: Paul Forrester

Typeset in Great Britain by
Central Southern Typesetters, Eastbourne
Manufactured in Singapore by Eray Scan Pte Ltd
Printed in China by Leefung-Asco Printers Ltd

ACKNOWLEDGMENTS

The author would like to thank the following people for the loan of their artwork:
Alex Douglas Morris, Adrianne Cross,
Charles Penny and Jim Russel

Contents

INTRODUCTION

Framing is a wonderful craft, and one of its great appeals is that it takes so little time to learn how to make a simple frame. With only a couple of pieces of wood and some glass you can make a present for a friend or a frame for a favourite photograph that is ready to hang on the wall within minutes.

Once you have mastered the basic techniques, you will find that there are endless possibilities, and the time taken perfecting the various aspects of the craft is very satisfying. The frame is important because any picture needs to be confined within a clearly defined area. When there is no frame, the eye tends to wander and it is difficult to focus on the image and to appreciate it properly. It is essential that the frame enhances the picture without overpowering it. The finishing edge – that is, the mount and the frame – should complement the picture but they must never be so intrusive that they are the first thing you look at. The frame is there to protect the work and to give it its own space within its surroundings. The finishing edge must ensure that the eye travels easily to the focal point of the picture.

There are no hard and fast rules that must be observed when you are choosing colours for the mounts and mouldings. Some people seem to have a knack for selecting the perfect combinations of shades; others learn as they go along. You may find it helpful to visit art galleries, museums and shops to look at the ways different frames and mouldings can be used to create different effects and how the various materials can be used to enhance the pictures they surround. If you look at Victorian watercolours, for example, you will see how the overall balance is maintained by the use of light ivory or cream-coloured mounts, often decorated with wash lines, together with a fairly dark wooden or deep gold frame. In general, a dark mount will look best with a lighter frame. Photographs, for instance, look good in smaller, darker mounts, with a narrow aluminium or silver-coloured frame.

Traditional framing has a long and rich history, but new products, which make techniques such as gilding and distressing so much easier than they used to be, have changed people's attitudes to the craft and encouraged new fashions. For example, at present a wood and paint finish is popular, and this technique is explained later in the book.

Equipment and Techniques

You need only a few tools to get started and you can even begin, as I did, by working on the sitting-room floor. If you are lucky, you will find that you already have most of the tools and equipment you will need in your household tool cupboard. There are, however, two items that you will probably have to buy – a mitre box or clamp and a mount cutter – but, in general you should think about buying new tools only as you need them, rather than acquiring them all at once.

Framing

To make the frames described in this book you will need the following:

- ◊ Pin hammer
- ◊ Tenon saw
- ◊ Screwdriver
- ◊ Pincers/pliers
- ◊ Nail punch
- ◊ Set square
- ◊ Hand drill and bits
- ◊ Panel pins
- ◊ Mitre box or clamp
- ◊ Metal ruler
- ◊ Plastic ruler and pencil
- ◊ Craft knife
- ◊ Wood glue

Mouldings

There is an enormous range of mouldings available to the amateur framer these days, but the main problem is finding shops that supply what you need and want. Some manufacturers operate a mail-order service, and you will find their names and addresses in craft magazines. A timber merchant may keep a few mouldings in stock, and your local picture framer may also be persuaded to help. When you are choosing a moulding, consider the size of the picture and such aspects as whether it is boldly coloured or finely drawn.

Because hard wood has become much scarcer in recent years, plastic mouldings have been introduced. These have the great advantages that they do not warp or suffer from woodworm. They also take gilding and coloured finishes well, although they do not, of course, have the wonderful smell and feel of real wood.

Moulding Formula

- This simple formula can be used to work out fairly accurately how much moulding you will need. Add together:
  The height of the picture x 2
  The width of the picture x 2
  The width across the top of the frame (ie of the moulding) x 8
  You need the additional width of the moulding for the mitre cuts that are made at the ends of each of the four pieces.
  For example, say that you are framing a picture measuring 31 x 25cm (12 x 10in) and that the depth of the moulding is 1cm (½in):
  31cm (12in) x 2 = 62cm (24in)
  25cm (10in) x 2 = 50cm (20in)
  1cm (½in) x 8 = 8cm (4in)
  = 120cm (48in)
  Add an extra 5cm (2in) to be on the safe side, and this means that you will need 125cm (50in) in total.

Using the Clamp and Saw

When your saw is new you may find that a little oil will make it run smoothly when you are cutting moulding. Try not to put a lot of pressure on the saw when you are cutting. Aim to use short, light, even strokes and to let the saw do the work. When it is not being used, always keep the saw in its cover to protect the teeth.

1

2

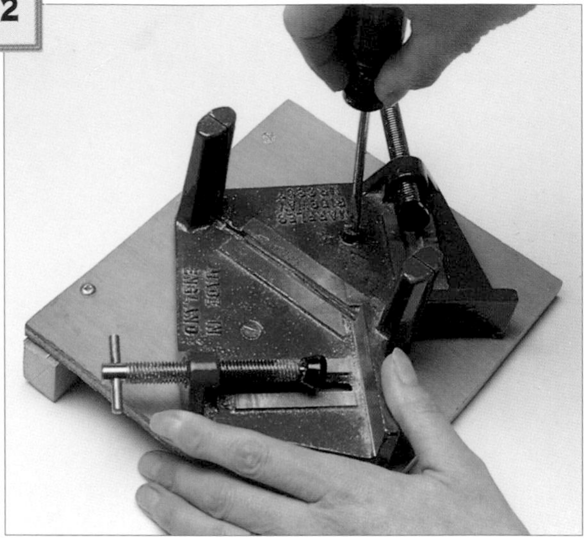

1 The clamp needs to be fixed to a wooden base. You will need a piece of 1cm (½in) plywood measuring about 20 x 18cm (8 x 7in). Cut a length of 3.5 x 2.5cm (1½ x 1in) timber to 20cm (8in) and screw it along the longer side of the piece of plywood to form a lip that will butt up against the edge of your working surface.

2 Screw the metal mitre clamp on to the plywood base so that the lip is on the other side.

3 Before you use a clamp for the first time, you may find it helpful to draw a line on the rubber insert of the base of the clamp to indicate the central cutting line.

Using a Mitre Clamp

- Make sure that the moulding is sitting flat on the base before you tighten up the screws.
- Use small pieces of card or off-cuts of wood at the end of the clamp screws to protect the moulding from any damage.
- If the base moves around too much when you are sawing pieces of wood, use a clamp to hold the base firmly to your working surface.
- When you have cut a corner and you need to smooth the edges, gently rub the cut edge on the rough side of some hardboard instead of using sandpaper, which may be too severe.

3

Using Corner Clamps

Frame corner clamps held with a cord are available, although they can be rather fiddly and awkward to work with. They can be useful, however, especially if you are making small or very narrow frames that are difficult to pin.

Take the four cut pieces of the frame and glue the ends of the long sides. Lay the frame on your working surface in the correct position and put the four corner clamps in place. Pull up the string until it is very tight, clean off any glue that has seeped out from the joints and put to one side until the glue is dry. There are several different types of frame corner clamps available.

Mounting

Your choice of mount can affect the final appearance of the painting even more than the frame itself. If the mount is too small it can appear to squeeze and confine the picture, so, at least at first, you should always make the mount slightly larger than you had originally planned.

You will need the following equipment to make the mounts described in this book:

◊ Cutting mat
◊ Mount cutter with ruler
◊ Compasses
◊ Pencil
◊ Adhesive tape
◊ Plastic ruler and pencil
◊ Scissors
◊ Craft knife
◊ Mapping pen and paint brush

You must make sure that the blade of your mount cutter is sharp. Keep a supply of spare blades and replace the worn one as often as necessary, but certainly every 5 or 6 mounts. Dispose of the old blade carefully.

Remember that the bottom edge of the mount is usually deeper than the top and sides, which should be the same depth. For example, if the top and sides were 8cm (3⅛in) deep, the bottom should be 10cm (4in) deep. This difference helps to lead the eye into the picture.

There is a huge range of mounting boards and cards available – the selection is so wide, in fact, that it can be rather confusing.

In general you should choose a light colour, especially if you are framing a watercolour painting. Pick an appropriate colour from the painting itself and match the tone of the colour with a light green, soft brown, ivory, cream and so on. If the colour seems too bland when it is surrounding the picture, wash or crayon lines can be added to draw the eye to the painting. A brightly coloured painting may look best with a pale mount but with a more vividly coloured frame.

There are several kinds of mount, and it is important to select the appropriate kind for the image you are framing. The different types are:

◊ A normal window mount
◊ A double mount, in which about 1cm (½in) of the colour of the underlying mount can be seen around the edge of the top mount
◊ A float, in which the picture lies on a coloured mount with 2–3cm (about 1in) of the mount showing all round the edge of the picture
◊ A float and mount combined, in which the picture lies on the lower mount while the window in the top mount is cut to reveal 1–2cm (about ½in) of the bottom mount around the picture
◊ Fabric covered mounts, when silk or hessian is used over the mount
◊ Paper-covered mounts
◊ Wash mounts

These are just a few of the possible mounting methods and materials. If you take care with the mount, choosing it thoughtfully and cutting it precisely, it will make all the difference to the final look of the picture.

Being sepia, this photograph has been treated like a drawing, and so has a large mount. Generally, however, they can often look swamped if the mount is too large, and they generally look best in small, dark mounts.

Prints require special treatment. If they are original, they will have a plate mark impressed on the paper, all around the image. The window of the mount should be sufficiently large for the plate mark to be visible, which usually means leaving a margin of white about 1cm (½in) wide around the actual printed image.

Double Wood Frame

This is the ideal frame for small pictures such as photographs or postcards. Because the fine inner frame is used in combination with a wider outer frame, the picture can be shown to advantage without having to use a mount.

You will need
◊ Narrow wood moulding (see page 5 for estimating quantity)
◊ Plastic ruler and pencil
◊ Mitre cutter and clamp
◊ Saw
◊ Craft knife
◊ Wood glue
◊ Drill and fine bit
◊ Panel pins
◊ Small hammer
◊ Wide wood moulding but with no rebate (see page 5 for estimating quantity)
◊ Nail punch
◊ White emulsion
◊ Acrylic paints
◊ 2mm (1/16in) glass
◊ T-square
◊ Felt-tipped pen
◊ Glass cutter
◊ 2mm (1/16in) hardboard
◊ Screw eyes
◊ Wire or card

1

1 Measure the photograph and assemble the frame from the narrow moulding as described in the Basic Frame (see page 14).

2

2 Use the completed inner frame to determine the dimensions of the outside frame. This is made from timber with no rebate. We used timber that was 30 x 5mm (1¼ x ¼in).

3

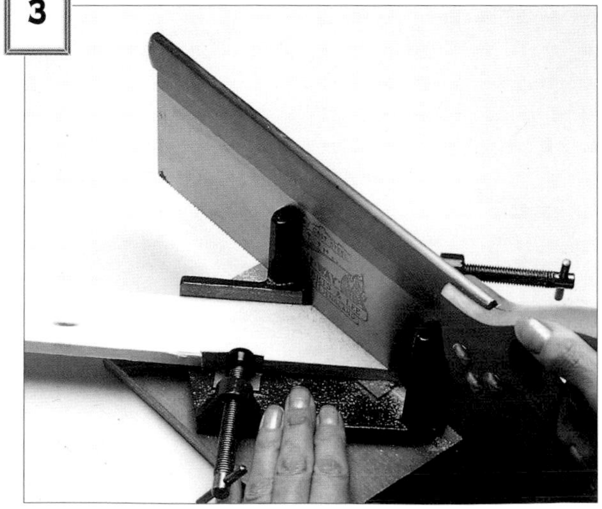

3 Make the first mitre cut, then make the two long sides and the short sides as described in the instructions for the Glass and Clip Frame (see page 20). Again this moulding has no rebate.

4 Glue and clamp the first corner together, then drill holes for the panel pins; we used 25mm (1in) pins, but you must use a size that will hold both pieces of wood securely. Use a nail punch to drive the pins in straight.

5 Paint the frames. Use contrasting colours for the frames, mixing acrylic paints with white emulsion until you find shades you like. Experiment on pieces of scrap wood before you paint the frame itself.

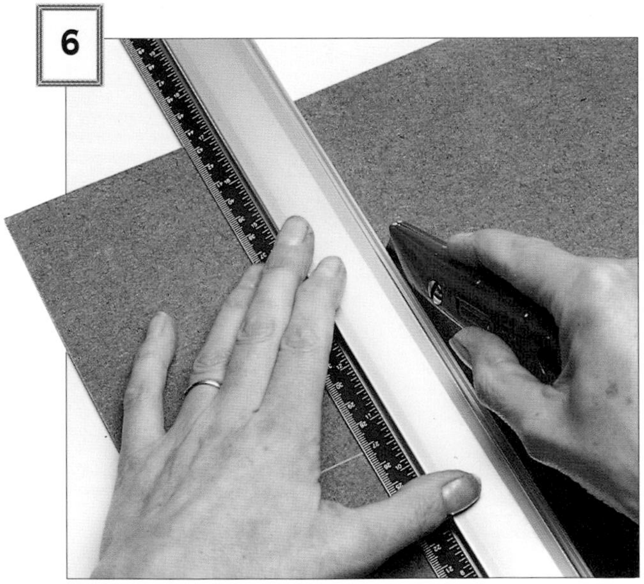

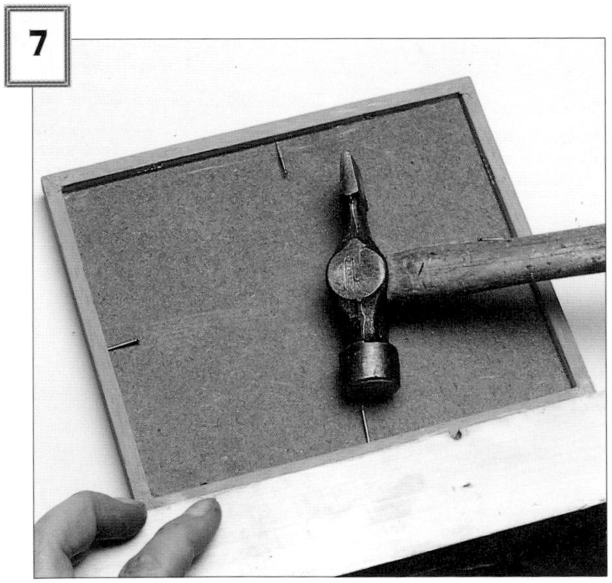

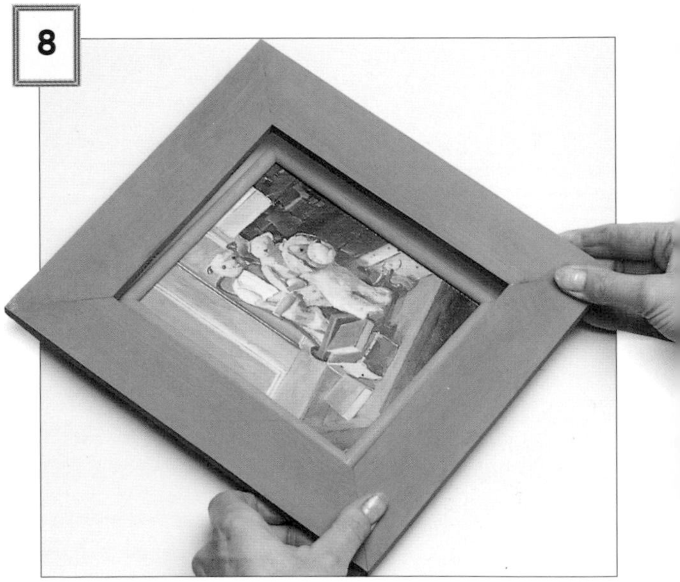

6 Cut the glass and a piece of hardboard to size, using the inner frame as a guide as to the dimensions. Fit the glass, picture, hardboard and inner frame together.

7 Hold the hardboard in place by driving some panel pins carefully into the edge of the inner frame.

8 Apply wood glue to the inside edge of the outer frame and push the inner frame through from the back. It should fit neatly. Insert the screw eyes and attach the wire so that you can hang your picture up.

Box Frame

This kind of frame is useful for holding three-dimensional objects such as a piece of embroidery or collectable items such as badges or medals. There are several ways of making box frames, but this is a simple and effective method. The size of the frame is determined by the backing board, which can be covered with coloured card or with polyester wadding and fabric. We have made the frame to display an arrangement of dried flowers mounted on card.

You will need
◊ Hardboard
◊ Plastic ruler and pencil
◊ Craft knife
◊ Polyester wadding
◊ Scissors
◊ Fabric
◊ Clear, all-purpose adhesive
◊ 2.5cm (1in) hockey wood moulding (see page 5 for estimating quantity)
◊ Mitre cutter and clamp
◊ Saw
◊ Wood glue
◊ Drill and fine bit
◊ Panel pins
◊ Small hammer
◊ 2mm (1/16in) glass
◊ Glass cutter
◊ T-square
◊ Card
◊ Masking tape or brown gummed paper
◊ Screw eyes
◊ Wire or cord

1

2

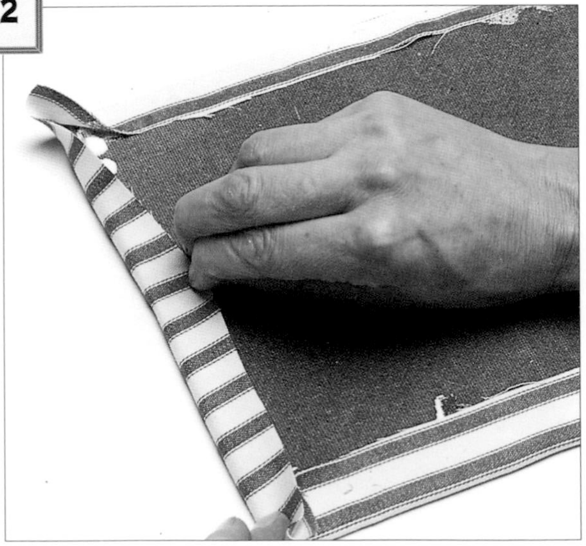

3

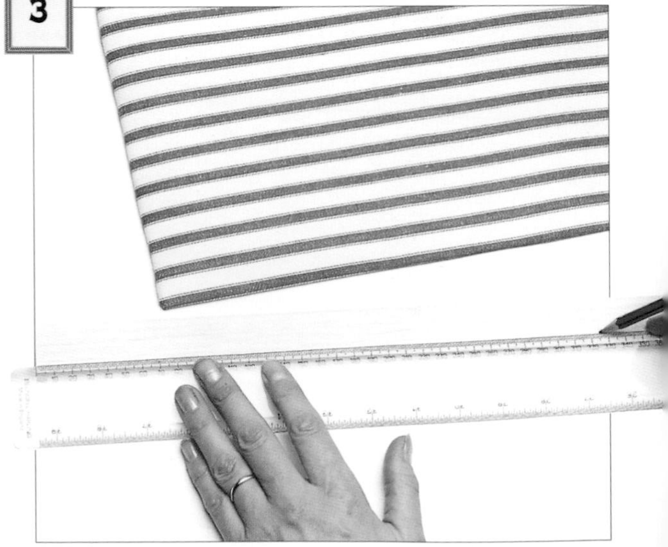

1 Cut a piece of hardboard to size – we used a piece that is 32.5 x 21.5cm (12½ x 8½in). Cover the hardboard with polyester wadding and cut a piece of fabric that is about 10mm (½in) larger all round than the hardboard.

2 Stretch the fabric over the wadding and glue it firmly to the back, making sure that the corners are neatly mitred.

3 Cut the first mitre in the moulding and, working on a long side first, measure the covered hardboard. Transfer this measurement to the outside edge of the moulding, measuring from one corner to the other.

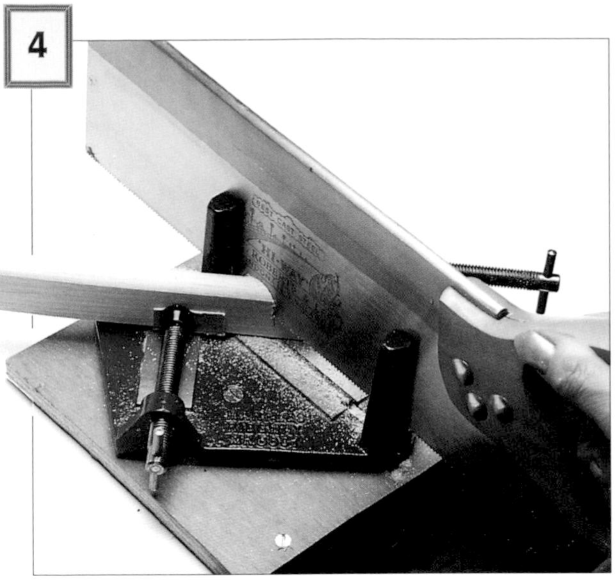

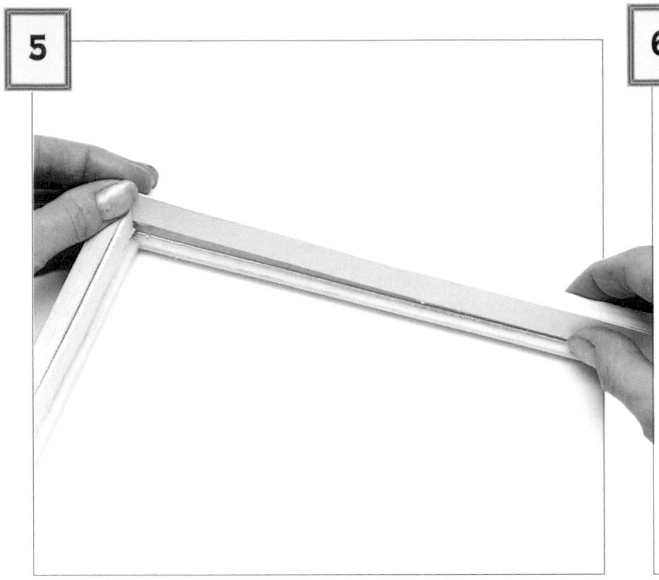

4 Slide the moulding into the mitre clamp and align the mark with the centre line of the vice. Cut the remaining three sides and assemble the frame as described in the instructions for the Basic Frame (see page 14). Once the frame is complete, cut a piece of glass to fit neatly inside the frame. Lay the frame face down on the table, clean the glass carefully and fit it into the frame.

5 Measure the depth of the side from the glass to the back of the frame – in our frame this was 20mm (about ¾in) – and cut four strips of thick card to this width and long enough to fit along the inside of the frame. Glue them in place, sticking the long pieces down first. These strips of card will hold the glass in position at the front of the box.

6 Attach the object or objects to the covered backing board. We used all-purpose adhesive to hold the card in place.

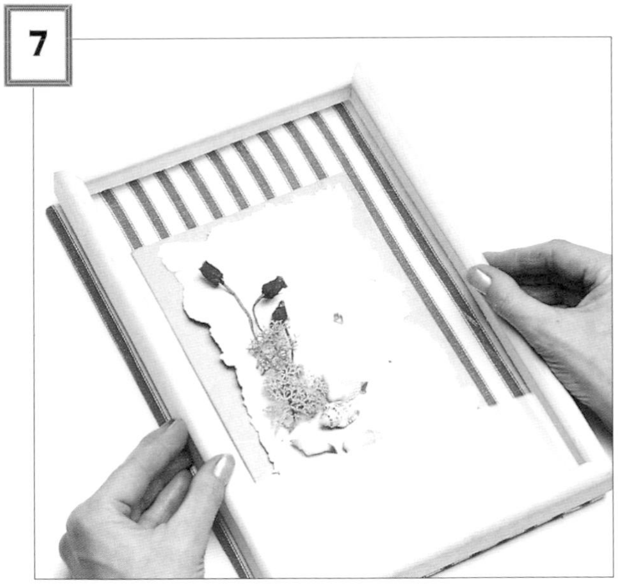

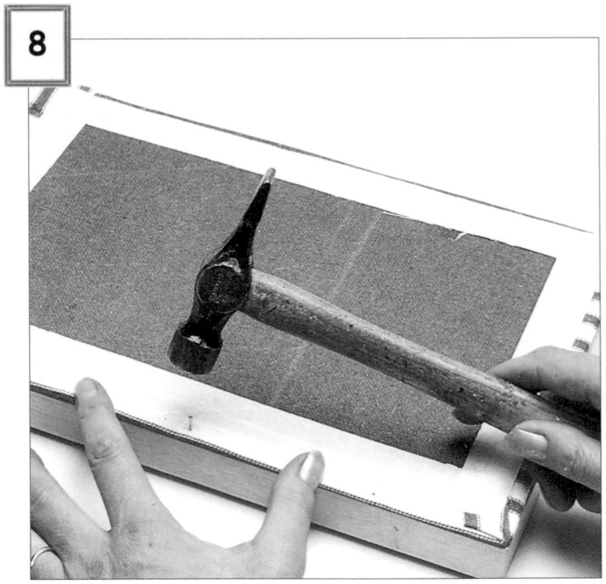

7 Place the frame over the backing board and carefully over the box.

8 Use small panel pins, tapped through the backing board into the frame, to hold the back in place. Cover the join with strips of masking tape or brown gummed paper.

9 With your hand drill, make holes, about one-third of the way down, on each side of the frame and insert the screw eyes. Attach wire or cord for hanging.

Shell Frame

If you have an old wooden frame that has seen better days, you can completely revitalize it by covering it with shells, feathers or even small bits of seaweed. Alternatively you can make your own frame, although you will need to use a fairly flat moulding or one that has only a gentle curve.

You will need
◊ Wooden frame
◊ White emulsion paint
◊ Acrylic paint
◊ Wire wool or a rag
◊ White candle (optional for wax resist)
◊ Screw eyes
◊ Mirror
◊ Panel pins and hammer
◊ Masking tape or gummed brown paper
◊ Strong adhesive
◊ Interior wall filler (optional for curved frame)
◊ Gold paint

1

2

1 If the frame is going to be painted, apply a coat of white emulsion and leave to dry.

2 Mix the acrylic paint, diluting it with a little emulsion to give a smooth, runny consistency. Experiment until you have a shade you like. Paint the frame and before the paint is completely dry use wire wool or a rag to drag some of the paint off.

3

3 An alternative method is to use the end of a candle to draw patterns on the dried base coat.

4

4 When you apply the acrylic paint, the wax will resist the paint and leave the white base coat showing through.

5

5 Screw the eyes into the back of the frame and, if you wish, insert the mirror, holding it in place with small panel pins. Cover the join with masking tape or gummed paper. Use a fairly strong adhesive to stick the shells and other ornaments into position. If the frame has a very uneven profile you may find it easier to mix a small amount of interior wall filler to press the shells into.

6 When you are happy with the final arrangement of the shells, add a touch of gold tube paint to create highlights on the shells, wiping off any excess before it dries.

6

REVIVING AN OLD FRAME

You might come across an attractive old frame in a junk shop or on a second-hand stall, but, when you get it home you realise that not only is it in a worse state than you at first thought but it also will not fit the picture you intended to put in it. You can use your newly acquired skills to take the frame apart and re-make it with new glass so that it fits perfectly.

You will need
◊ Pliers
◊ Hammer
◊ Screwdriver
◊ Plastic ruler and pencil
◊ Mitre cutter and clamp
◊ Saw
◊ Craft knife
◊ Wood glue
◊ Drill and fine bit
◊ Panel pins
◊ Fine wire wool
◊ Emulsion paint
◊ Gold paint (in liquid, powder or tube form)
◊ 2mm (1/16in) glass
◊ Glass cutter
◊ T-square
◊ Masking tape or brown gummed paper
◊ Screw eyes
◊ Wire or cord

1

1 First remove the backing and the glass from the old frame. Take care because the glass may be old and fragile. Stand the frame on a corner, hold the opposite corner and gently push down until the corners crack.

TIP

- If the frame is an old wooden one, always sand and stain it before applying a wax finish.
- Make a plain frame by applying two coats of a solid, dark paint.

2

3

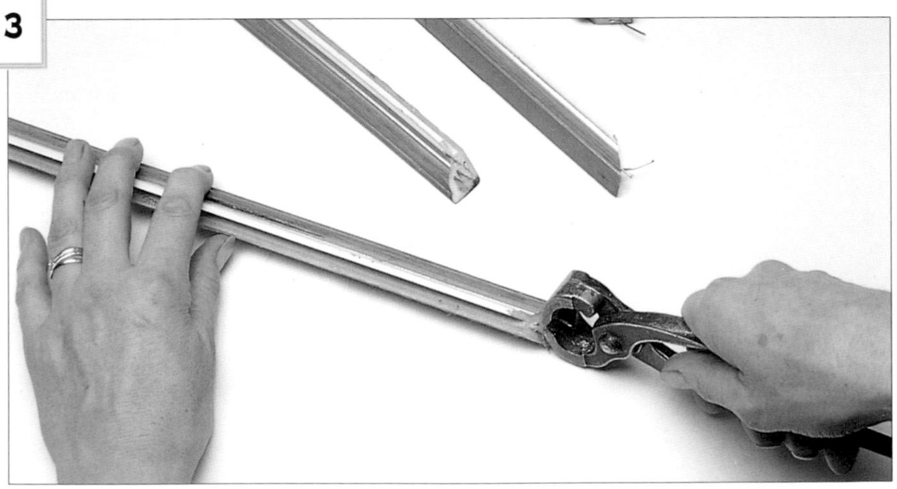

2 If pins have been used, push the sides apart and wiggle them apart. If the frame has been underpinned, use a screwdriver and hammer to drive the pins out.

3 Once the frame is in pieces, use your pliers to remove any remaining pins. Working on one of the long sides, cut a new mitred corner.

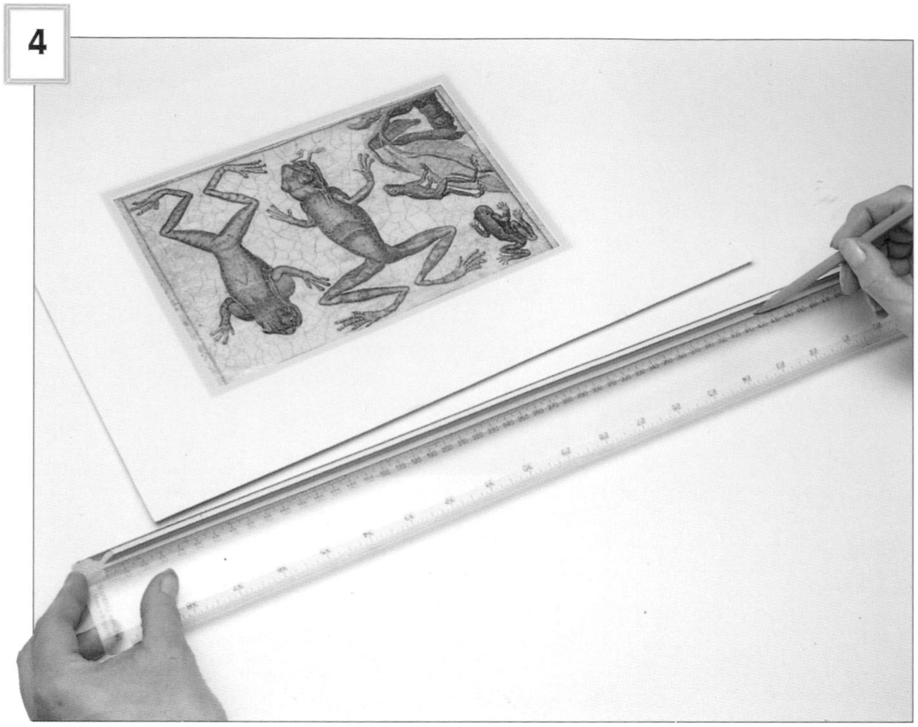

4 Measure the long side of the picture you want to frame and transfer the measurement to the inside of the newly cut side.

5 Slide the moulding into the mitre clamp and align the mark with the centre cutting line. Cut all the sides as for the Basic Frame (see page 14) and re-assemble the pieces.

6 You can now decorate the frame, choosing a style that is in keeping with the picture that is going in it. We have used an old print of some frogs and want the frame to look suitably distressed and aged. To achieve this appearance, rub the frame all over with fine wire wool.

7 Apply a coat of dark brick-red emulsion all over the frame. Leave to dry. You may need to apply a second coat if the first did not cover the frame completely.

8 When the paint is dry, smooth it carefully with fine wire wool, then apply a coat of liquid gold leaf or another proprietary gold paint. Some gold powders need to be mixed with shellac or button polish, so always check the manufacturer's instructions.

9 When the gold paint is dry, rub it gently with fine wire wool to give a distressed look, with the red paint showing through in places. Insert the glass and finish off the frame as described in the instructions for the Basic Frame (see page 18).

Papier-Mâché Frame

Making this frame for a mirror will allow you to combine your framing skills with the satisfying craft of papier-mâché. We have created a simple design, with fish swimming around the glass, although this is a technique that allows you to give your creative talents full rein.

You will need

◊ 1 x 1cm (½ x ½in) plain wooden moulding (see page 5 for estimating quantity)
◊ Plastic ruler and pencil
◊ Mitre cutter and clamp
◊ Saw
◊ Craft knife
◊ Wood glue
◊ Drill and fine bit
◊ Panel pins
◊ Small hammer
◊ Tracing paper
◊ Mounting card or thick card
◊ Scraps of newspaper, torn into small pieces
◊ Masking tape
◊ Flour-and-water paste or wallpaper paste
◊ Masking tape or brown gummed paper
◊ Acrylic glue (optional)
◊ Clear, all-purpose adhesive
◊ White tissue paper
◊ Acrylic paint
◊ Polyurethane
◊ Screw eyes
◊ Wire or cord

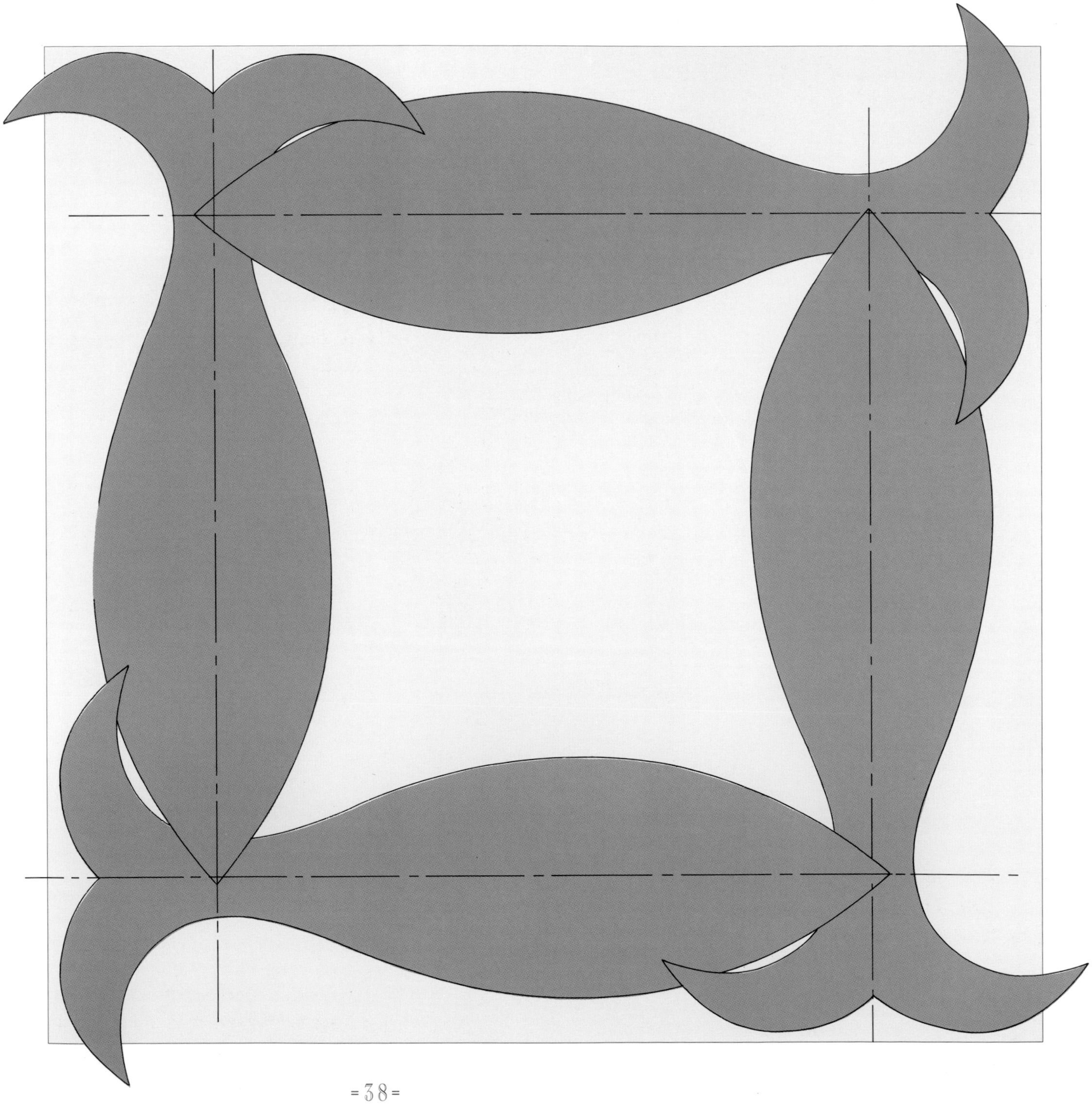

1

1 Use the wooden moulding to make a three-sided frame, following the instructions for the Basic Frame (see page 14). We have made a square frame, measuring 16.5 x 16.5cm (6½ x 6½in). Leave the opening at the top so that you can slip in the mirror.

2

2 Trace the fish design (or a motif of your choice) onto a spare piece of card. Use a craft knife to cut out four fish shapes.

3

3 Tear up some pieces of newspaper and scrunch them up loosely. Use tape to hold them onto the parts of the fish bodies that you want to be fuller and more rounded.

4

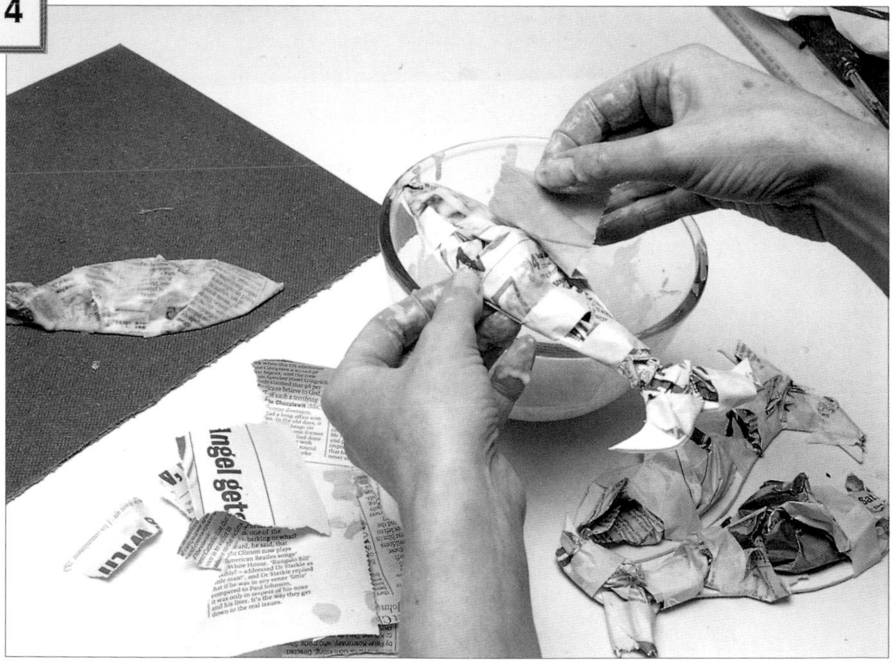

4 Mix the paste. If you use flour-and-water paste you can add a small amount of acrylic glue to make it stronger. Dip pieces of paper into the paste and begin to cover the fish bodies. Do not let the paper become saturated with paste, and if you find that the paper is too wet, lay some dry pieces over the shapes. When you are satisfied with the overall shapes, smooth the surface of each fish and leave them somewhere warm until they are absolutely dry.

5

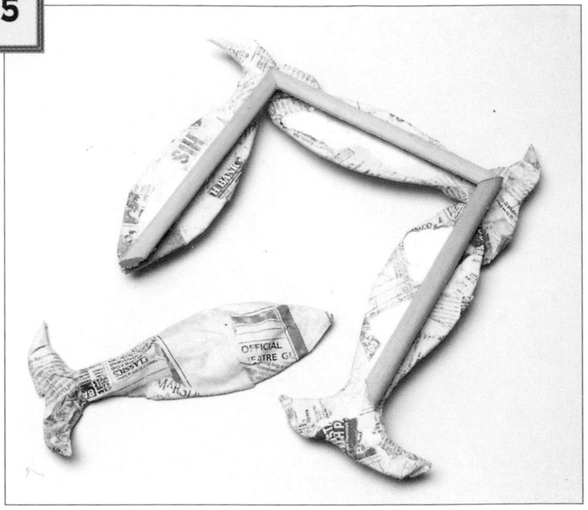

5 Take the frame and arrange the fish on it. When you are satisfied with the positions they are in, use a lot of adhesive to stick them, nose to tail, around the frame.

6

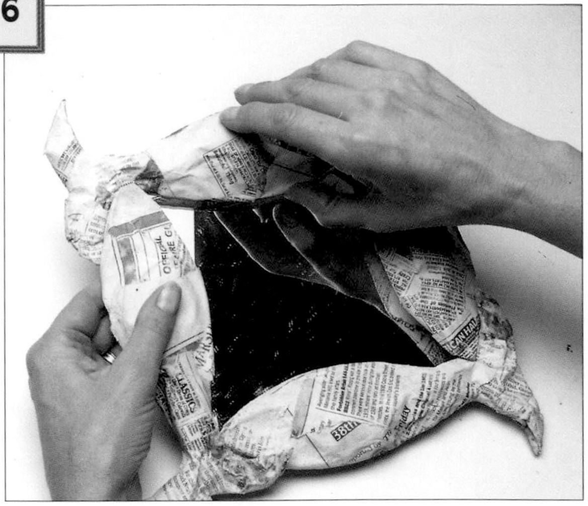

6 The fish at the top should be attached by its nose and tail. Place under a weight and leave until the adhesive is dry. Check that the mirror will slide into the frame, but do not leave it there yet. Add more layers of papier-mâché to the fish, using strips of paper across the back of the top fish to make sure it is firmly attached to its neighbours. Put back in a warm place to dry.

7

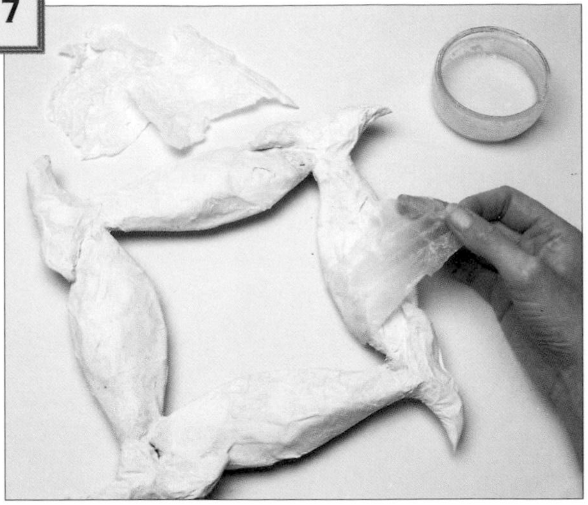

7 To finish the fish, cover them completely with two layers of white tissue paper. The colours of the paint will be much brighter and clearer if they are applied over a white base.

8

8 When the fish are dry, paint them in colours of your choice. Leave the paint to dry, then apply a coat of clear polyurethane.

9

9 Insert the mirror and apply screw eyes on the sides to hang up the frame.

Gilded and Painted Frame

Naive paintings and prints usually have a strong image, often in good, clear colours, and they do not usually need a mount if they are in a wide frame. We have chosen to frame a print of a sheep, which measures 40 x 30.5cm (16 x 12in). This frame can either be simply painted or it can be finished with gold to give it extra sparkle.

You will need

◊ Moulding (see page 5 for estimating quantity)
◊ Mitre cutter and clamp
◊ Saw
◊ Plastic ruler and pencil
◊ Wood glue
◊ Drill and fine bit
◊ Panel pins
◊ Small hammer
◊ Nail punch
◊ Shellac and paintbrush (optional)
◊ Red emulsion paint
◊ Fine wire wool
◊ Masking tape
◊ Emulsion and acrylic paints
◊ Gold paint (in liquid, powder or tube form)
◊ Shoe polish and soft cloth (optional)
◊ Metal gold leaf and size
◊ Soft, long-handled brush

1

1 Make the frame in the moulding of your choice, following the instructions for the Basic Frame (see page 14). If you wish, seal the wood by applying a coat of shellac. Apply two or three coats of red paint, leaving each coat to dry completely before you paint on the next. Gently rub the surface with fine wire wool.

TIP

• If you need to tone a colour down, add a little black acrylic paint rather than more of the base colour.

2

2 If you are going to have a gilded edge, apply strips of masking tape around the centre of the frame.

3

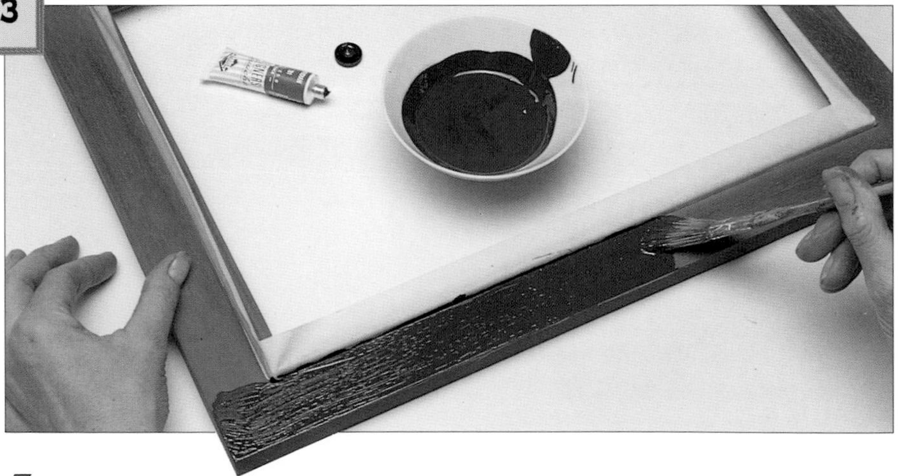

3 Mix the emulsion and acrylic paints. We used dark green, made by mixing green acrylic with a little white emulsion paint to give it body. Apply the paint to the outer edge of the frame, taking care that it does not seep under the masking tape.

4 When the paint is completely dry, rub it gently with wire wool to distress it. If you wish you can leave the frame as it is.

5 If you want to add a gold edge, remove the masking tape and put new strips of tape over the area you have just painted. Following the manufacturer's instructions for the gold paint you are using, paint the edge of the frame and leave this to dry.

6 If you want the gold to look "aged", apply a tiny amount of dark shoe polish and rub it carefully with a soft cloth. If you prefer, use wire wool to remove part of the gold to give an even more distressed appearance.

7 If you prefer, you can apply quick gilding with metal gold leaf, which is quick and easy to use. Apply fresh strips of masking tape as in step 5. Working on small sections of the frame, apply some gilding size and wait until it becomes tacky.

8

8 Cut a piece of gold leaf large enough to cover the edge and leave the paper backing on it. Use your fingertips to carefully position the gold leaf and to press it down gently.

9

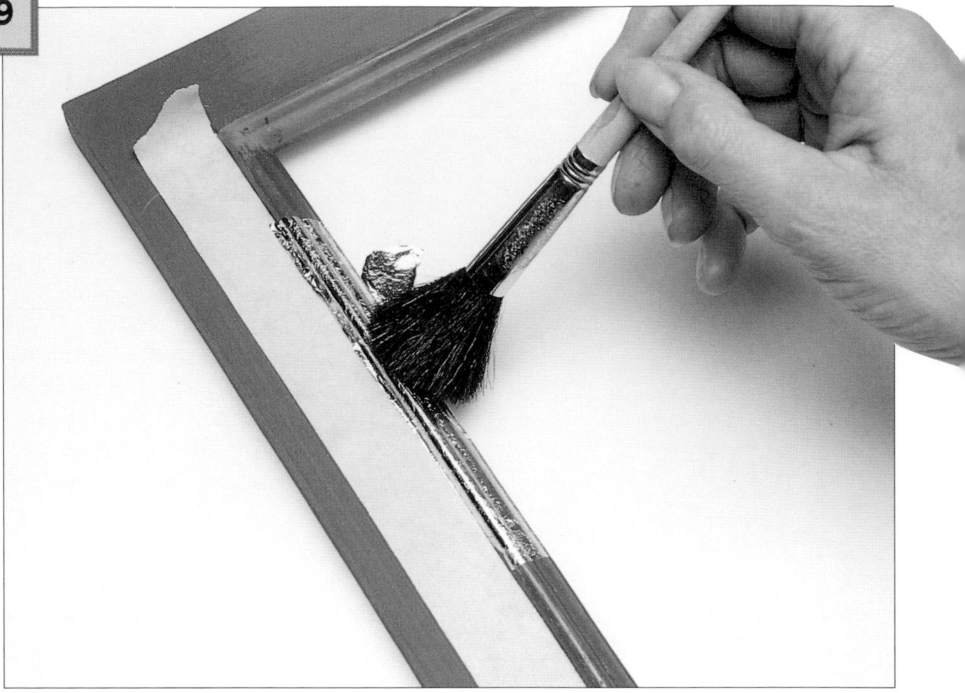

9 You may find it helpful to use a soft brush to make sure you have pressed it down completely. Carefully remove the backing paper.

10

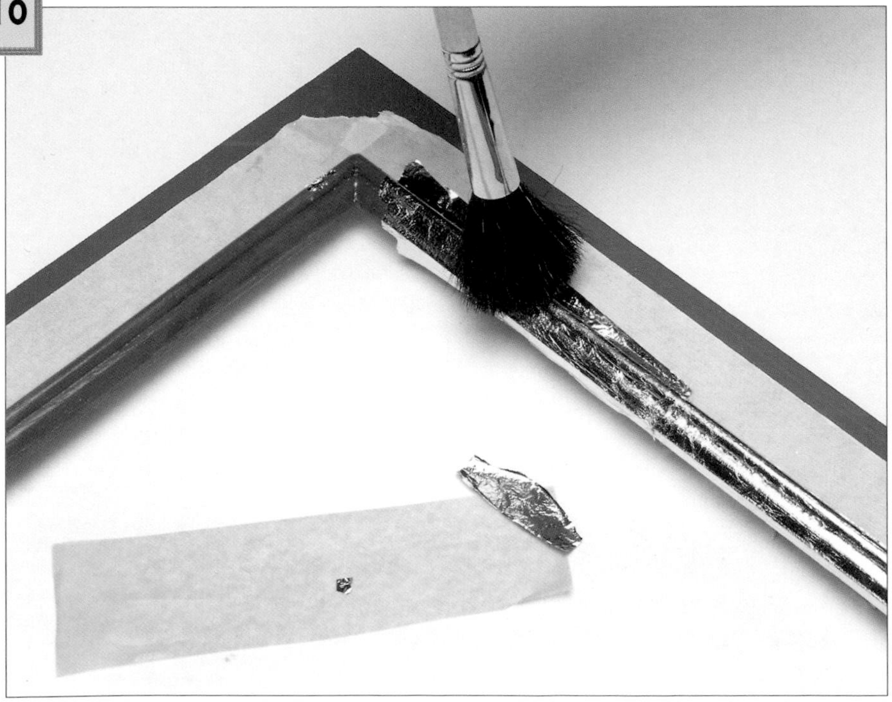

10 Continue to work around the frame, overlapping the gold leaf by about 3mm (⅛in) each time. If you find you have missed any, use small scraps of gold leaf to cover the gaps or, when the size has dried completely, use gold paint to fill in the gaps. Use a soft, long-handled brush to remove any loose particles.

11

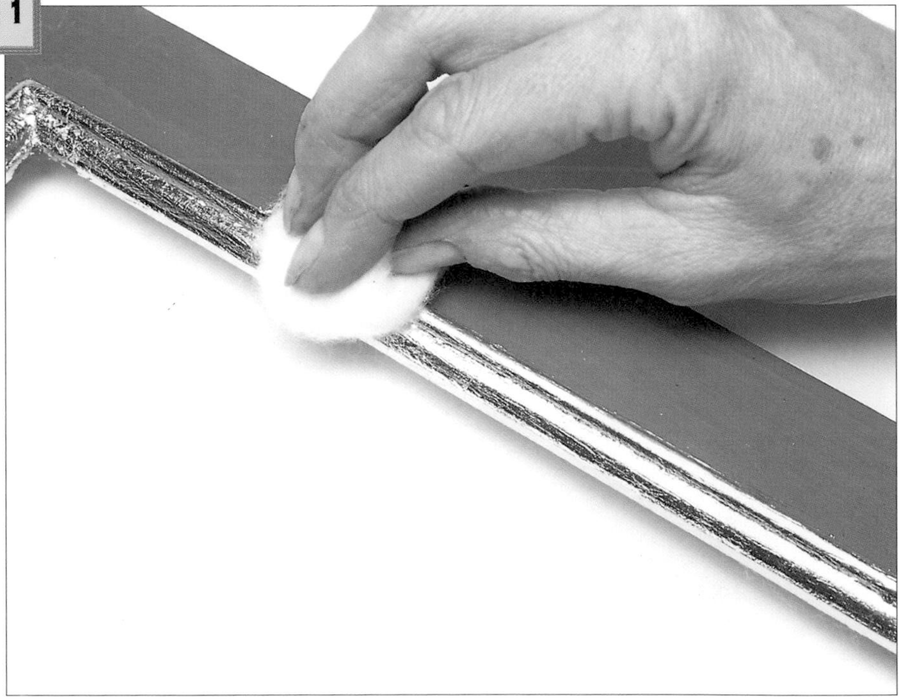

11 Leave to dry for a few hours or, ideally, overnight until the size is quite dry. Use a ball of cotton wool to buff the gold leaf until it gleams.

TIP

- When it comes to the corners, take care not to overlap the gold leaf too much, otherwise they will be very bulky. Again, use a soft brush to remove loose particles.

FRAMING AN OIL PAINTING

Oil paintings need to be treated rather differently from prints and watercolours, but it is still important to have a space between the image and the frame. A simple way of doing this is to float the painting on a board covered in a material such as hessian or coarse linen. The fabric is stretched taut over hardboard and the painting is fixed to the covered board. An alternative method, which we are using, is to make an inner slip and an outside frame. The slip can be wood, gold or silver or, as we used, linen, and it serves the additional purpose of holding the glass slightly away from the surface of the painting if you choose to glaze it, although traditionally oil paintings are not glazed.

You will need

◊ Ruler and pencil
◊ Linen slip moulding (see page 5 for estimating quantity)
◊ Masking tape
◊ Mitre cutter and clamp
◊ Saw
◊ Wood glue
◊ Drill and fine bit
◊ Panel pins
◊ Small hammer
◊ Nail punch
◊ Outer moulding (see page 5 for estimating quantity)
◊ D-rings or screw eyes
◊ Wire or cord

1 Measure the painting. Ours was 58.5 x 43cm (23 x 17in). Working on the long measurement first, add about 3mm (⅛in) and cut a piece of linen slip moulding to this length. To protect the linen and to stop it from tearing, cover the cutting area with masking tape before cutting.

1

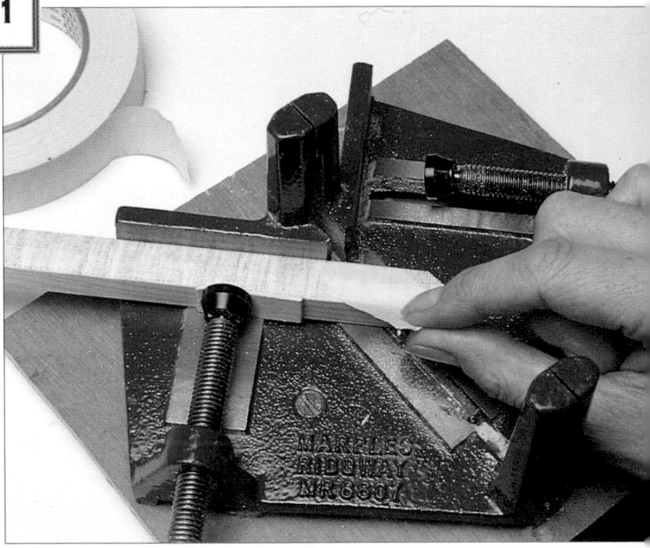

2

2 Follow the instructions for making the Basic Frame (see page 14), but before you drill the holes for the panel pins lay the pieces around the oil painting, holding them together in position to check that the frame will fit. Oil paintings are not always perfectly square and you may need to make some fine adjustments.

3 Finish off the frame as described on page 18. Use a nail punch to drive the panel pins into the corners, making sure that they are securely held.

3

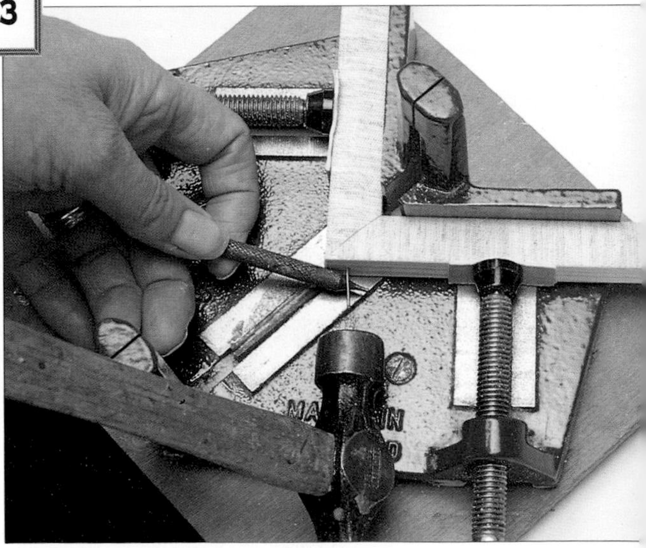

4

4 Make the outer frame, using the inner frame as a guide to mark the measurements. Do not allow any extra because the frames should fit tightly together. Make the outer frame as the inner frame.

5

5 Fit the oil painting into the slip frame and carefully insert panel pins to hold it in place. Place the outer frame over the slip frame. Pin the back by driving panel pins in upright then tapping them until they bend over. You will need about two pins along each side.

6

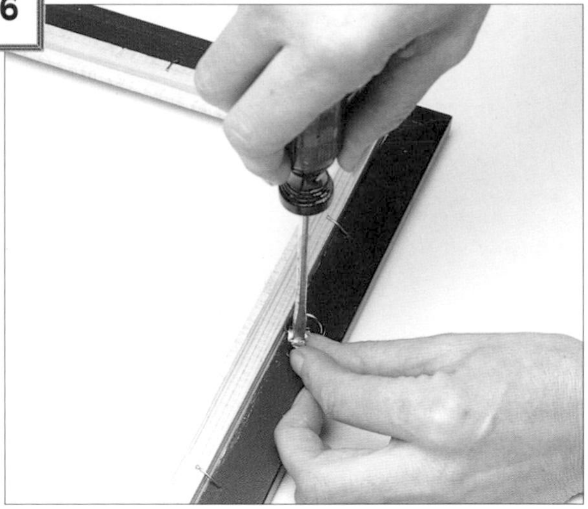

6 Make holes for the screw eyes or D-rings on each side of the outer frame.

GLOSSARY

Acid Free: This is the term used to describe card, mountboard and tape that is made free from acid, and which ensures that the artwork you are framing does not become marked or damaged over a length of time.

Bevel: The sloping cut edge of a mount.

Bole: A clay applied over gesso as a base for goldleafing. Can also be used on its own.

Distressing: Making a gold leaf or painted frame look old by rubbing through to the base colour with wire wool.

Double mount: Two mounts one on top of the other. The window of the top mount is larger than that of the bottom mount.

Float: A piece of mountcard is cut approximately 1in or 2.5cm larger than the artwork. Centre the artwork onto the card and it floats with card showing all the way round.

Gesso: Chalk whiting and size which is used in layers to build up a base for gold leaf and other finishes.

Limed wood: Wood treated with a wash of white paint, lime paste or limed wax.

Mitre: A 45° angle used on moulding to make the corners of the frame.

Mitre box: A metal or wooden box used for cutting the 45° angle on the moulding.

Moulding: Specially turned wood with a rebate used for framing.

Mount or Mat: Card with a window in it that helps you hang and protect the artwork.

Rebate: The recess on the inside of a piece of moulding into which all the parts of the picture are fitted.

Ruling or mapping pen: A pen that has two parallel blunt nibs. When filled with watercolour or ink, it is used to draw wash lines on mounts.

Score: To mark a line on a piece of card or glass with a cutting tool to enable you to bend the card or sever the glass.

Wash: A layer of thinned paint, usually watercolour, used to acquire a translucent and delicate effect. Used in between wash lines, mainly for watercolours.

Window: The hole cut in a mount, through which you can see the painting.